An Introduc
Critical Thinking and
Writing
in American Politics

Wadsworth Publishing Company
I(T)P® An International Thomson Publishing Company

Belmont, CA • Albany, NY • Bonn • Boston • Cincinnati
Detroit • Johannesburg • London • Madrid • Melbourne • Mexico City
New York • Paris • Singapore • Tokyo • Toronto • Washington

COPYRIGHT © 1998 by Wadsworth Publishing Company
A Division of International Thomson Publishing Inc.
I(T)P® The ITP logo is a registered trademark under license.

Printed in the United States of America
1 2 3 4 5 6 7 8 9 10

For more information, contact Wadsworth Publishing Company,
10 Davis Drive, Belmont, CA 94002, or electronically at
http://www.thomson.com/wadsworth.html

International Thomson
Publishing Europe
Berkshire House 168-173
High Holborn
London, WC1V 7AA, England

International Thomson
Publishing GmbH
Königswinterer Strasse 418
53227 Bonn, Germany

Thomas Nelson Australia
102 Dodds Street
South Melbourne 3205
Victoria, Australia

International Thomson
Publishing Asia
221 Henderson Rd.
#05-10 Henderson Building
Singapore 0315

Nelson Canada
1120 Birchmount Road
Scarborough, Ontario
Canada M1K 5G4

International Thomson
Publishing Japan
Hirakawacho Kyowa bldg, 3F
2-2-1 Hirakawacho
Chiyoda-ku, Tokyo 102, Japan

International Thomson
Publishing Southern Africa
Building 18, Constantia Park
240 Old Pretoria Road
Halfway House, 1685 South Africa

International Thomson
Editores
Campos Eliseos 385, Piso 7
Col Polanco
11560 México D.F. México

All rights reserved. No part of this work covered by the copyright hereon
may be reproduced or used in any form or by any means—graphic,
electronic, or mechanical, including photocopying, recording, taping, or
information storage and retrieval systems—without the written
permission of the publisher.

ISBN 0-534-53634-4

Introduction

Most students think that taking lecture notes and memorizing them, as well as reading a textbook and memorizing the important facts therein, are the keys to success in the classroom. But in order truly to learn from your course in American government, politics, or political science, you need to be able to think critically about American politics. Critical-thinking techniques, in addition to being applicable to political arguments, also are important to virtually all disciplines, such as economics, sociology, psychology, marketing, and ethics, to name a few. Additionally, critical thinking can be a valuable tool in daily life because it involves making judgments and decisions based on information. Critical thinking involves the examination of information from different sources.

In this Handbook, designed to accompany *American Government and Politics Today* and *American Government and Politics Today: The Essentials*, we present strategies in critical thinking that will allow you to make better use of the information that you receive about the political sphere. Using the techniques described in this booklet will help you to separate reality from rhetoric regarding the information you obtain from television, radio, newspapers, political campaign speeches, government publications, and privately sponsored publications. Throughout the pages that follow, we use examples that relate specifically to American politics. You should be able, nonetheless, to use the methodology of critical thinking presented here in all of your courses as well as in your day-to-day activities.

Equally important to success in the classroom—and in any human enterprise—is the ability to communicate your knowledge to others. Most instructors have their students do at least some writing in their courses because they know that critical thinking and communication skills go hand in hand. In effect, thinking and writing are part of the same learning process. Whenever you are required to express what you have learned in writing—whether it be in an essay exam, a term paper, or an article for a newspaper—you are forced to clarify and organize logically your thoughts on the subject. In so doing, you quickly learn just what you do, and do not, know about a topic. If you are like most people, you have probably had the experience of assuming that you understood a concept quite clearly—only to find out, when putting pen to paper, that the concept was actually quite fuzzy in your mind. To be able to express and justify in writing the conclusions you have drawn after a critical evaluation of source materials is, in a sense, the ultimate "test" of clear, critical thinking.

If you are required to submit a research paper, you may find the prospect daunting. Writing a successful research paper is never easy, even for the most advanced scholar. To ease your task and help you make the best use of your time, we conclude this *Handbook* with some general guidelines on writing a successful research paper.

Defining Critical Thinking

Critical thinking involves the capacity to distinguish beliefs from knowledge, and fact from judgment. Someone skilled in critical thinking is able to analyze, criticize, and advocate ideas. He or she can also draw factual or judgmental conclusions based on inferences drawn from either unambiguous statements of knowledge or personal beliefs. When a critical thinker makes a judgmental conclusion that is based in whole or in part on a personal belief, he or she should understand the extent to which the belief has influenced his or her judgment.

All of the above is a fancy way of saying that a person should find good reasons to reject or support an argument. This means that *the critical thinker first defines the problem, then examines the evidence, and always analyzes the assumptions underlying the evidence.* Critical thinking is incomplete without considering alternative interpretations. Finally, the implications of different interpretations must also be recognized.

Critical thinking, more than anything else, is adopting an attitude that is open to both sides of an argument while proceeding with what might be called *intellectual caution.* Additionally, the critical thinker has to be prepared to accept defeat, which may involve

having one's own cherished beliefs blown to smith-
ereens by someone else's better-reasoned and
factually more correct argument.

Critical thinking requires active participation in
the learning process. Rather than reading every word
we've written in our text, *American Government and
Politics Today* and *American Government and Politics
Today: The Essentials*, and accepting it at face value,
you, as a critical-thinking student, must take an active role in questioning our conclusions and those of
your instructor. This brings us to our first rule in
critical thinking.

Critical Thinking Rule 1: Engage in Active Information Acquisition

Don't be a passive acquirer of information. Don't
just sit in the classroom and take down every word the
instructor says. Don't read a textbook and accept everything in it as "the truth." Critical thinking requires
active questioning of most information that is offered.
While you are taking notes in class, jot down in the
margins questions about the lecturer's information.
The same holds true when reading this and all other
textbooks. For example, surveys on the religious
beliefs of Americans are reported regularly. The
Gallup poll, in particular, gives the results of people's
attitudes about religion. In the last decade, those
polls showed that over 30 percent of adult Americans
fit a particular definition of "evangelicals." If you are
an *active* acquirer of information, you will immediately

question that relatively high percentage: it means that one out of three American adults claims to be an evangelical. If the percentage didn't seem high when you read it the first time, you were not engaging in critical thinking. In order to understand why the statistic is so high you must dig further into the underpinnings of the survey. Typically, the Gallup poll's definition of "evangelical" is extremely broad, for it includes those who describe themselves as "born-again Christians," as well as those who claim to encourage others to believe in Jesus Christ. Additionally, virtually anybody who said he or she interprets the Bible literally is typically considered an evangelical by such polls.

Deriving conclusions based on what people say presents us with our second rule of critical thinking.

Critical Thinking Rule 2: Be Suspicious of Individuals' Self-reports of Their Own Attitudes

Although scientific poll-taking has been developed through the years to such a point that most polls are relatively accurate, individuals' self-reports about their attitudes may not reflect accurately how they really feel. One place to start when examining opinion polls regarding American politics and other fields is by asking yourself the question: "Is the subject matter of the poll something that individuals have to act on? If they do, is there any direct personal cost involved?"

Consider an example. A polling organization wants to determine who will win the next presidential election. The pollsters can ask a very simple question of all the individuals interviewed: "Who are you going to vote for?" In this situation, the individuals polled have to go vote in order to carry out what they said they were going to do. The cost involved is only the time and trouble of going to a voting location on election day. Perhaps a large number of individuals polled (if they had any opinion at all) would carry out their promised action by voting for one candidate or the other.

Now consider another example: improvement of public mass transportation in a particular city. If pollsters simply went out and interviewed people on the street, asking the question "Do you think there should be better public mass transportation?", the results probably would show overwhelmingly that most people interviewed want better public mass transportation. But ask yourself some critical questions about such interview techniques: Did the individuals who were polled have to think about the cost of the improvements? How many would support new taxes to pay for better mass transit? In this example, most individuals interviewed probably did not think they would pay anything to solve the problem.

A general corollary to Critical Thinking Rule 2 comes out of this discussion: If individuals think they won't have to pay for something or give anything up for something beneficial to occur, on average they will be in favor of it occurring. That is why opinion polls about increased benefits from governmental actions have to be viewed with a critical eye. Unless the pollsters also ask specific questions about how much individuals are willing to pay for better public mass transportation (or any other service), the poll results

6

should be viewed cautiously.

It is one thing to ask citizens if they want their public mass transportation system improved and quite another to inquire if they are willing to pay increased taxes or to reduce monies from a competing social or defense program to pay for the new system.

Critical Thinking Rule 3: Don't Jump to Conclusions

It is very easy for individuals to jump to a conclusion with just a smattering of evidence or logic. To avoid jumping to conclusions, you have to look at the following:

a. The evidence.
b. The specificity of the argument; is it too general?
c. Is there any alternative explanation (observational equivalence)?

Examine the Evidence

Unless one is dealing in pure logic in a philosophy course, most arguments involving hypotheses about how the political world works must be accompanied by some evidence to be convincing. When you examine arguments in our text or listen to them from your instructor, constantly ask "What is the evidence?" Then ask yourself "Is there more evidence?" Consider the bureaucracy chapter in *American Government and Politics Today* and *American Government and Politics*

7

Today: The Essentials. Notice that the chapter on bureaucracy is included in the part of the book that concerns political institutions. These institutions include the Congress, presidency, and judiciary. If you examine the United States Constitution, only the Congress, presidency, and judiciary are mentioned. The bureaucracy is not, yet it is considered the "fourth branch of government." Thus, implicit in the placement of the chapter on the bureaucracy in that part that concerns political institutions is the assumption that it should be examined along with the three formal branches of our government. Does the evidence presented in the chapter justify its placement in that part of the textbook? Is the federal bureaucracy the fourth branch of government? How much of the evidence in the chapter on bureaucracy is persuasive about this issue? Consider one datum: About 15 percent of the entire civilian population over the age of sixteen works directly for the government. Does that bit of evidence convince you? It shouldn't, because we don't know how much power that specific 15 percent of the population has over our lives. If 100 percent of the government workers merely cleaned streets, then we would be hard-pressed to believe that such a group had any power.

The point in this subsection is that any issue demands evidence. You have to be aware of the possibility of not knowing all the evidence.

Specificity of the Argument

Is it possible that what you are reading or hearing is a generalization? Many political arguments result in over-generalizations that do not hold in many situations. Consider some examples. The generalized view of Republicans versus Democrats is that Republicans are pro-business, fiscally conservative, and opposed to high levels of government activity. This generalization is derived from a mixture of data, the reading of the Republican party platforms during presidential campaigns, and constant reinforcement in the rhetoric of Republican candidates and office holders.

But such a generalization does not work well if data covering a lengthy time span are examined. One appropriate set of data includes a comparison of the amount of "red ink" that each administration has incurred for the nation. Red ink is another name for a federal government deficit—an excess of federal government spending over federal government revenues, which are mainly derived from taxes on individuals and corporations.

Consider the period prior to the Great Depression, during the administration of Herbert Hoover, through the end of the Bush Administration in 1992. There were six Republican presidents: Hoover, Eisenhower, Nixon, Ford, Reagan, and Bush. They had four years of surpluses and twenty-six years of deficits (red ink). The five Democrat presidents (Roosevelt, Truman, Kennedy, Johnson, and Carter) had five surpluses and twenty-seven deficits. It looks like the generalization is barely true, doesn't it? The Democrats had one more year of federal government deficits than the Republicans. But the story doesn't end there. We have to look at the *cumulative* budget deficits during each president's term expressed as a percentage of the nation's output of goods and services. When we do, we find that, except for Roosevelt's administration, which included World War II, Demo-

9

cratic administrations, on average, have gone in the red less than Republican administrations. In fact, since the Great Depression (except for Roosevelt's terms of office) the Reagan and Bush administrations had the all-time high in federal government deficits. Indeed, the increase to our national debt during Reagan's eight years exceeded all of the debts (including World War II) that all administrations had created, beginning with that of George Washington.

Alternative Explanations

Many arguments are presented that sound logically correct and seem to have evidence to support them. The problem is that alternative explanations may be available. In the theory of scientific methodology, when such a situation occurs we call it a case of *observationally equivalent* hypotheses.

Take an example that is available virtually every day in the newspaper—what happened to the stock market yesterday. Almost every business page or every radio or television news commentator has something to say about what happened to the price of stocks yesterday. If the stock market went down yesterday, business commentators will cite various reasons—the dollar weakened; there was an increased threat of war in the Middle East; a threat of the steel unions going on strike; or something else. If the stock market went up yesterday, commentators might say that it is because the latest index of inflation showed that it was falling, the price of oil went down, or the president got over a cold. Unfortunately, none of those explanations, neither the evidence presented nor by the logical nature of the arguments or supporting arguments, is observationally distinguishable from any other explanation offered. There are many alternative explanations about why the stock market went up or down yesterday. Merely stating something that sounds logical means absolutely nothing.

To explain why stock prices went up or down yesterday involves much more than stating something that sounds plausible. There are at least 100 plausible explanations of why stocks changed price yesterday. Only by focusing on a limited number of explanations, testing those explanations scientifically, and examining lots of evidence can we even hope to come up with an hypothesis that is not observationally equivalent to a dozen other hypotheses.

Critical Thinking Rule 4: Beware of Tautologies, or Truisms

A problem similar to the one of observational equivalence of explanations about why something happens involves tautologies, or truisms. A *tautology*, or *truism*, is a statement that is always true. For example, if you ask what the weather is going to be tomorrow, we could state: It is either going to rain or it is not going to rain. That is a tautology, or truism. It is always a correct statement. Moreover, such a statement can never be disproved by any data. If the data show that it rained, we have confirmed the statement; if it didn't rain, we have also confirmed the statement.

Think about one element of the foundation of the American creed: In the United States, all men and

11

women are created equal. The sentiment behind this statement is certainly one that many Americans support as an ideal, but saying it does not make it true. Regardless of what the Declaration of Independence says, the evidence from the real world shows that some boy and girl babies are certainly *not* born equal to others. Their parents may be teenagers, unemployed, drug users, or lack a high school education. Believing that all men and women are created equal because a political culture endorses the statement is a classic example of a truism.

A critical thinker must avoid tautologies, or truisms. They may be great for light cocktail-party conversations, but they do not help you, as a critical thinker, get a better understanding about the world around you. When you start listening critically, particularly to people's casual conversations, you may be surprised at how many of the statements made are merely tautologies.

Critical Thinking Rule 5: Correlation is Not the Same as Causation

Lots of facts in the real world seem to be correlated. That is to say, the movement in one variable appears to mirror the movement in another, or appears to be opposite of the movement in another. We all know the correlation between regularly eating too much and gaining weight. There seems to be a correlation between smoking and contracting lung disease. The world is literally filled with correlations. *But statistical correlation is not equivalent to causation.*

Causation occurs when a change in one variable *causes* a change in another. There is a correlation between the number of days of sunshine and plant growth. Causation also seems to be implied here. That is to say, a change in the number of sunny days causes a change in the same direction in the growth rate of plants. There are scientific ways to prove such causation. They typically involve setting up a model in which sunlight is an independent variable (along with others, such as water consumption, fertilizer, etc.) and plant growth is the dependent variable.

In American politics, there are numerous correlations that can be discovered. Typically, election analysts would expect to find correlations between being African American and voting Democratic, being wealthy and voting Republican, and being young and not voting at all. Although certain demographic traits are correlated or associated with voting patterns, these are not all *causal* explanations. Being under 30 does not cause non-voting; rather, the transient lifestyle of younger Americans and their lack of attachment to a community and family both work to keep them away from the polls.

Consider another example. Every president elected in a year ending with the number zero, from William Henry Harrison in 1840 to John F. Kennedy in 1960, has died in office. The correlation is between years ending in zero and presidential death. It seems quite clear, however, that presidential death was not *caused* by the years ending in zero. Instead this is one of those strange coincidences (called *spurious correlations*) in American politics.

In contrast, some political correlations may in fact turn out to be causal relationships. The question

13

of why we have only two major parties, as explained in your text's chapter on political parties, is one which can be answered by a causal theory. The impact of election laws that favor only the major parties combines with the winner-take-all rules to make the two-party system inevitable. Evidence from the experiences of other nations support this causal relationship.

Consider also that higher proportions of people with more years of college education vote in national elections in the United States. More education is related to voting because education *causes* increased levels of efficacy, the feeling that one's political views are valuable and should be expressed.

Many other correlations have nothing to do with causation. To take an absurd example, without an hypothesis behind the correlation between smoking and lung cancer, we could just as easily say that lung cancer causes smoking. Now that sounds absurd, but someone could come up with a theory in which the growth of cancerous cells in the body at a very young age, although undetectable, affect people's psyches and make them want to smoke. Sounds crazy, doesn't it? But it could be supported by the same set of correlational data that support the opposite causal theory that smoking causes lung cancer.

In sum, in order to think critically you must not draw conclusions about causation from information that is simply correlational. Correlational findings—A is associated with B—can be interpreted in two ways. Unless you have a good theory about the *direction* of causation about which condition occurred first, you can't even begin to use correlational findings to help you understand how the political world (or any other) really works.

This brings us to a related rule in critical thinking concerning alternative explanations.

Critical Thinking Rule 6: Avoid Over-Simplification by Considering Alternative Explanations

Every critical thinker avoids over-simplification. While all explanations of the real world require some simplification, there must be a limit. Typically, over-simplifications result from brief examinations of findings that are correlational. Suppose that somebody showed you the dates of the last three wars and the party affiliation of the presidents in office when those wars started. If two out of the three administrations were Democratic, could you jump to the conclusion that Democrats cause wars? Hardly. Even if we ignore that you haven't started out with a theory about why Democratic administrations would be more prone to engage in war, you have over-simplified because (1) you haven't thought of alternative explanations of the correlational findings, and (2) you haven't looked at enough evidence. This country has had more than three wars, so you would at least want to look at the data from all of the wars in which the U.S. was engaged. And then you would still have to decide whether there were enough data to reach a conclusion about which administrations were more prone to engage this country in war.

One way to avoid over-simplifications is to try to go beyond what most people take at face value, or to go

15

beyond the obvious.

Critical Thinking Rule 7: Go Beyond the Obvious: Discover What Variables Created the Observed Phenomenon

To continue the example from above, if you truly want to find out whether Democrats or Republicans engage in more wars, go beyond simple correlational findings and examine the underlying forces that actually caused each war. There haven't been that many in our history, so the task would not be too difficult.

First of all one should point out that there were wars fought by Americans before a Democratic was elected president (the war of 1812, for example). When World War II broke out there were many factors at play, in addition to a Democratic administration, which are much more likely to explain American involvement in that war. They were:

- the defeat and humiliation of Germany in World War I

- the hyperinflation that destroyed the German economy in the 1920s

- a worldwide economic depression during the 1930s

- the rise of fascism and militarism in Italy, Germany, and Japan

- the Japanese bombing of Pearl Harbor on December 7, 1941

As far as the Vietnam War is concerned, American involvement really began with the Republican Eisenhower administration. Moreover, for many centuries, Vietnam had been engaged in wars with neighboring states. After World War II the French were embroiled in that part of the world, which was then called Indochina. American involvement actually began as a U.S. effort to help France fight its war. American involvement gradually expanded during the Democratic administrations of Kennedy and Johnson, and also under the Republican Nixon administration.

We can turn to the sphere of domestic politics for yet another example going beyond the obvious. If wheat sells for $5.00 a bushel, one could assume that the price is set by supply and demand. If, however, you look more closely at the policies which regulate the prices of wheat, tobacco, milk, sugar, and other products, you will find that these agricultural products are price-supported by the U.S. government because of the pressure of producer-interest groups.

Critical Thinking Rule 8: Poke Holes in all Arguments-- Even Your Own!

A critical thinker always attempts to poke holes in every argument, even his or her own. This is particularly true when you are examining generalizations. Consider a common one: Democratic administrations are anti-business and Republican administrations favor business over people. This has at various times been a common generalization about one of the differences between the two major parties in the United States. It's relatively easy to poke holes in this generalization by looking at some history. Under Democratic President John F. Kennedy, businesses received the single largest tax break in the history of the United States. Under Republican President Richard M. Nixon, more economic controls were put on the business community in the form of nationwide wage and price controls than under any other administration (except during war time). There you have it: two exceptions to the generalization about Democrats being anti-business and Republicans being pro-business.

Your job as a critical thinker is constantly to question the arguments, data, causal theories, correlations, generalizations, and all-encompassing statements about how the world works.

Critical Thinking Rule 9: Realize What Your Value Judgments Are

Each of us has a set of values and therefore a set of value judgments about everything that we consider, whether we know it or not. Our values are formed by our parents, peers, schools, the books we read, our religious concepts, the movies we see, and a thousand other variables. A critical thinker can never change his or her past inputs, but every critical thinker can be aware of what his or her values are with respect to any given subject.

If you are examining arguments for and against abortion, your values may enter very strongly into your assessment of the validity of certain arguments and evidence. It is important that you are aware of how much your religious and family upbringing affect your views about what others say or write concerning this explosive topic.

If you are examining arguments for and against a new international trade bill that will impose higher costs on foreign companies attempting to sell their goods in the United States, you must ask yourself whether you have certain values that cause you to want to keep foreign competition out of the United States. Perhaps your values are such that you are basically xenophobic—you dislike anything foreign— or that you know someone who lost her job because of foreign competition. This brings us to another rule of critical thinking.

Critical Thinking Rule 10: Attempt to Conquer Your Biases

Biases and values are closely linked; our biases are the result of our values. They affect what we favor every time a situation affords us the power of choice. Of course, this carries over to our analyses of political issues. If you have a bias against individuals who live in a particular geographical location in the United

States, when you hear a politician from that area you may not listen to his or her words with complete objectivity. You must recognize your biases in order to see the objective points made by such a politician.

You may have a bias against rich or poor people; when you examine the arguments outlining the case for higher taxes for the rich, or increased welfare for the poor, you may not see through to the true argument because of your biases.

Critical Thinking Rule 11: Define Your Terms

How often have you argued with someone only to discover that you weren't talking about the same thing because each of you had a different definition of some key term? Consider an example. Someone tells you that poverty has increased during the last four presidential administrations. Can you argue effectively with anyone about poverty without defining what it means? You have to state an income that you consider to be at the poverty level. You also have to state that you are talking about poverty only in the United States. Only after such agreement can you discuss what actually has happened to poverty in this country.

The most debated definition of the 1992 presidential campaign was attached to the phrase "family values." Conservative Republicans such as Pat Buchanan, Dan Quayle, and Phillis Schlafly defined them as typified by a traditional two-parent family that lives together in which there is a female mother and a male father who are legally married, who have children and in which neither of the parents is a homosexual. Vice President Dan Quayle emphasized this definition when he criticized the television character Murphy Brown for having a child as a single mother. In addition to the actual structure of the family, conservatives emphasized values such as morality, religion, traditional male and female gender roles, discipline, prayer in schools, patriotism, and a pro-life philosophy. As far as policies to strengthen the family, conservative Republicans emphasized self sufficiency, "hard work," private enterprise and private initiative, plus law and order as the most desirable government policies.

Liberal and/or Democrats, in contrast, (including Bill and Hillary Clinton and Jesse Jackson) defined "family values" much more broadly in terms of, first of all, a household consisting of a wide variety of possible persons including traditional two-parent families, but also single parents and their child or children, gay/lesbian couples, persons living with each other who are not married or a combination of these. They stressed the fact that the traditional two-parent family is now the exception in the United States and that therefore all the other living arrangements must also be taken into account. Liberals and Democrats emphasized individuality, the affection of people in the family for each other—love, sharing, compassion, and commitment for each other. Policies that liberals and Democrats emphasized as ways to strengthen the family and build positive family values included expanded health, education, and housing programs, child care, greater rights and protection for gays, lesbians, and women (taking a tough stand against sexual harassment for example), more emphasis on job opportunities and rebuilding the inner cities to strengthen families under stress.

If you can define the ideas attached to such terms as "family values," "liberal," and "conservative," "pro-life," and "pro-choice," the terms can then be used by two or more individuals in a meaningful debate.

As an example, someone tells you that Bill Clinton won the 1992 election by a "landslide." What does "landslide" mean? What is the definition of that word? Who made up the definition? Was it Clinton's campaign chair? Was it Bush's campaign chair? Was it a reporter, TV anchor, or your local newspaper? Is there an official or at least an authoritative, unbiased source for defining the term? What, in your view, would be a good neutral source? Would a professor who has studied every election since 1850 be a good source?

Would you consider a landslide to be a presidential election in which the candidate wins 40 states and 400 electoral votes, 49 states and 500 electoral votes, or would you call it a landslide if a candidate obtained a large percent of the popular vote, say, 60 percent?

Another example is the claim that someone "won the debate?" For example, there was a televised "debate" between Vice President Al Gore and Ross Perot on *Larry King Live* in the fall of 1993. The subject matter was the North American Free Trade Act (NAFTA). It was said that Vice President Al Gore "won." Does this mean he had the best ideas and policies? Was his style of debating the most aggressive? Did he simply prove that he could face a political opponent for an hour without making a major mistake? Or did he follow all the technical rules and guidelines outlined in some book on debating and therefore won on technique? Did he "win" because he convinced a lot of TV viewers that the Clinton Administration's position on NAFTA was the best position?

Critical Thinking Rule 12: Beware of Prescriptive Arguments

Most arguments consist of an issue, reasons, and then a conclusion. That's the beginning, middle, and end of the argument; you either agree with the conclusion or don't. But some arguments go past that, and add a final conclusion that is not necessarily based on the first conclusion. These are called *prescriptive* arguments because they ask for action to be undertaken. In the political arena, prescriptive arguments are often presented. It is important to critical thinking that they are recognized as such. Consider someone trying to get a law passed to ban liquor advertising. This person starts with an issue such as teenage drunk driving. He points out that the data show that there has been a dramatic increase in deaths from teenage drunk driving. His conclusion is that in the United States, teenage drunk driving has become an increasingly serious problem. His next conclusion in this argument is a prescriptive one: "Therefore, I believe that all liquor advertising should be prohibited."

The recommendation to prohibit liquor advertising is an added conclusion that goes beyond the basic assertion that the problem of teenage drunk driving has worsened. Clearly one can agree with the

23

first conclusion teenage drunk driving has worsened without agreeing with the prescriptive conclusion indicating what type of legislative action should be undertaken as a remedy.

Another way of viewing the distinction between these types of arguments is to note that one is a *positive* argument while the other is *normative*. A positive argument states an issue, the facts, and a conclusion without any further prescriptive ideas. A normative argument includes a prescription about what should be done. Indeed, whenever you see or hear the word *should*, listen carefully for the normative argument that is being offered. Normative arguments rely almost solely on people's values.

Consider another example. Suppose that we give you the information that in the last two years the number of individuals reporting that they are unemployed has increased. We can all draw the conclusion that unemployment, therefore, is a worsening problem. That conclusion is in the realm of positive analysis. But if we add, "Therefore, unemployment benefits should be expanded and increased," we are telling you something from our heart. Our values have helped persuade us what should be done to rectify the situation. (In the realm of normative statements, normative means value-ladened.)

The critical thinker will always separate the positive from the normative aspects of any argument or set of arguments. Normative, or prescriptive, statements calling for action require separate analysis and understanding. You may reject a prescriptive conclusion because you do not accept the validity of a set of its supporting positive statements. Alternatively, you may reject a prescriptive conclusion merely because it does not comply with your system of values.

24

You may agree, for example, that there has been an increase in teenage drunk driving and that it is a horrible problem. But you may be unwilling to accept a ban on all liquor advertising because you believe such an action would violate manufacturers' freedom of commercial speech.

You do not have to accept any normative argument, but you should always be aware of why you reject it, and be able to state clearly why your values do not allow you to accept it.

Summary of Rules of Critical Thinking

1. Engage in active information acquisition.

2. Be suspicious of individuals' self-reports of their own attitudes.

3. Don't jump to conclusions.

4. Beware of tautologies, or truisms.

5. Remember that correlation is not the same as causation.

6. Avoid over-simplification by considering alternative explanations.

7. Go beyond the obvious: Discover what variables create the observed phenomenon.

8. Poke holes in all arguments—even your own.

9. Realize what your value judgments are.

10. Attempt to conquer your biases.

11. Define your terms.

12. Beware of prescriptive arguments.

HOW TO WRITE A SUCCESS-FUL RESEARCH PAPER

Writing a successful research paper involves two processes—research and writing. Critical thinking is essential to good research, and following the rules discussed above can help you arrive at valid and significant conclusions. But no matter how carefully and thoroughly you have researched a topic and analyzed the results, you cannot write a successful research paper unless you can communicate your conclusions to others in written form.

In the remaining pages of this *Handbook*, we offer some tips on how to write a successful research paper. The first two rules deal with topic selection and research strategy, both of which are important elements in determining how successful your research paper will be. The remaining rules concern the writing process itself. Unfortunately, most of us are not born with writing skills. We must acquire them. The writing rules offered in this section are offered only as guidelines to good writing—no more, no less. The cardinal precept that you should always keep foremost in mind is that good writing *communicates* something—an idea, a concept, or other information—to the reader. In writing a research paper, as in all writing, communication with your reader should be your constant goal.

The first rule in writing a successful research paper is to plan ahead when selecting your topic.

Writing Rule 1: Plan Ahead When Selecting Your Topic

Selecting your topic is by far the most important decision you will make during your entire project. By exercising some care and foresight at this stage of the game, you can save yourself a lot of wasted time and frustration later. First of all, select a topic that interests you. Bear in mind that you will be spending at least several weeks researching your topic. If your topic is dull and uninspiring, your research hours could be deadly. Moreover, if you are not interested in your topic, you will find it extremely hard to interest your reader in your topic when it comes time to write your research paper.

Second, limit your topic so that it is appropriate to the required length of your research paper and the time period in which you must complete the project. If you choose too broad a topic, you will have insufficient time to do the research necessary for significant conclusions. By definition, a research paper offers a contribution to scholarship; it contains new insights or new information. You need to limit your topic so that you can cover the relevant sources sufficiently in the time available.

Third, define your approach. How are you going to approach your subject? What will your "slant" be? What is your thesis? What do you want to prove or disprove? What will you be looking for during your

28

research? The clearer your focus from the outset, the easier your labors will be. Your research task will be simpler because you will have a better idea of which research sources are directly relevant and which are extraneous to your topic. Your writing task will be easier because your approach to your subject will provide the structural basis for your paper.

Once you have selected your topic, you need to develop a research strategy so that you will have sufficient time for writing your paper.

Writing Rule 2:
Develop a Research Strategy

Your first task in undertaking research is to locate the sources and materials that you need to study. In this effort, librarians can be your most useful allies. They can direct you immediately to the major bibliographies and general source works relevant to your topic. Once you get started, you will undoubtedly find an abundance of sources and materials that are related to your subject. You will also undoubtedly find that you cannot possibly study all of them in the time allotted. Do not be daunted by this fact. Time constraints are part of life—we all face them every day in nearly every undertaking, social or professional. Look ahead to the date when the paper is due and make a time management plan. Set aside several blocks of time for library work, first to narrow the topic and find major sources, then several sessions to gather data. Look at your calendar and decide when you will write the first drafts. Then allow time for revisions and polishing the paper before the final date. Resist the temptation to write it the night before. Part of doing research is acknowledging the fact that you are operating under a time constraint and are planning accordingly.

Adequate coverage of source materials is essential to valid research results. But how do you know when you have adequately covered the sources? How many of the relevant and available documents must you examine before you can draw valid conclusions? Ideally, of course, you would study every document or source available. But in all likelihood, this will be impossible, given your time constraint. As a general rule, if you have covered two-thirds of the relevant data, you will be sufficiently grounded in your area of study to know what is and is not significant and to make valid conclusions.

Once you have covered at least two-thirds of the available research sources and feel confident that you have discovered sufficient evidence to justify your conclusions, then consider turning to the other part of your project—writing the research paper. One of the pitfalls of writing a research paper is getting "lost in the library," as it were, and concentrating on continued research and analysis at the expense of writing. Remember that writing a good research paper takes time. Finding every item of data and covering every research source is a wonderful ideal, but don't let your aspirations toward perfection work against your primary goal: completing a research paper in a specified period of time. Be wary of falling victim to what some have termed the "analysis to paralysis" syndrome— analyzing data and documents until decision making becomes impossible. Knowing when to stop researching and start writing is essential to a good research strategy.

Writing Rule 3:
Create an Outline before
You Write

Before you start writing your paper, you will need to organize the results of your research and decide how to structure your presentation. The simplest way to do this is by creating an outline. The outline might consist of merely a few pencilled notes; or it might be a full-fledged, detailed outline of your research paper. Its form is less important than its function—which is to clarify your thoughts and organize your presentation.

When creating an outline, it is helpful to distance yourself from your research efforts and view your topic from a broader perspective. Ask yourself the kinds of questions that someone unfamiliar with your topic might ask: What exactly is your topic? Why did you choose to study it? What is your central argument, or thesis? What evidence supports your conclusions? Why are your conclusions meaningful or significant? How does your research study relate to other scholarships in the field? In what way are your conclusions distinguishable from those of others? Such questions will force you to focus on the basic purpose of your research and the major conclusions that you have drawn—which is what your reader will want to know.

At a minimum, your outline should indicate the central thesis or idea of your paper, the major points

31

you will be making in support of your central thesis or idea, the key data and sources supporting each major point, and your conclusion. The best outline will allow you to write your first draft without reference to your notes or other research sources. But don't let your outline constrain your writing. Think of your outline as a kind of temporary "road map" that shows your point of departure, the route you plan to take, and your destination. Remember that the purpose of your map is to get you to your destination as smoothly and swiftly as possible. If it ends up taking you over rough roads or steering you in the wrong direction, modify the map until it serves your goals.

Writing Rule 4:
Use a Word Processor, if Possible

If you don't own a microcomputer, try to find one to use in crafting your paper. Borrow one from a friend, if possible; if not, see if there is one available in the library. A microcomputer can save hours of your time, particularly when you have finished your first draft and begin to make revisions. Although a word processor won't do your writing for you, it allows you to move text around, add or change text, correct mis-spelled words, generate tables and graphic illustrations, change margins, and generally perform nearly all editing functions with little effort. Also, your finished product will be neat, easy to read, and attractive in appearance.

Although computers are a boon to writers, they

can also be a bane. They make revision so simple that it is tempting to revise endlessly. Guard against this temptation by taking your words seriously and only changing them if the change results in a definite improvement. Often, the first expression of an intuition or idea is the most accurate in the long run.

Writing Rule 5: Remember—A First Draft Is Only a First Draft

Generating your first draft will be the most difficult part of your writing project. Your task will be easier if you remember that a first draft is just that—a beginning draft. It is not your final word on the subject. Your first draft should be thought of as merely a first stab at getting your thoughts on paper. At this stage, the important thing is to put your ideas on paper quickly and without a great deal of agony. Don't worry about spelling, sophisticated terminology, correct syntax, weak transitions, stylistic devices, and so on during your first draft. Once you begin to write your first draft, try not to stop. Follow your outline and let your ideas flow. If you reach a point at which you need to refer to your notes, leave a gap in your text to be filled in later and proceed with your next paragraph or section. The important thing is to commit your ideas to paper. Awkward text or disjointed paragraphs and sections can be repaired later when you edit and polish your draft.

Once you have completed your first draft, read through it—aloud, if possible—and identify any prob-

33

lem areas. Examine your conclusions closely in light of the rules on critical thinking that were discussed earlier in this *Handbook*. Have you jumped to any conclusions? Have personal biases affected your conclusions in any significant way? Have you overlooked important variables that could affect the validity of your conclusions? To write confidently about your conclusions, you need to be certain that they are accurate and justified. Once you are satisfied that the substance of your paper is sound, then you can turn to the task of editing and revising your paper.

Writing Rule 6: Allow Plenty of Time for Revisions

Excellent research papers read smoothly, clearly, and persuasively. They are set in an aesthetically pleasing format; they are free of grammatical and spelling errors; and they reveal an appropriate, careful choice of words. They do not "lose" the reader in clumsy, confusing, or overly lengthy or boring sentences. Neither do they jar the reader's senses by a series of short, staccato-like statements. Sentences, paragraphs, and sections flow smoothly and logically from one to the other. No point is understated or overstated. The paper concludes at the right time on just the right note. Obviously, all of these qualities cannot be achieved on a first draft, even by the most clever, experienced writer. They require extensive, time-consuming revision. When planning your writing schedule, allow plenty of time for revising your first draft.

When revising your paper, apply Writing Rules 7 to 12 to your writing. Change and correct your text as necessary in view of these rules. Also, have a dictionary, a handbook on English grammar and usage, a style manual, and a thesaurus close at hand. Use them. Careful revision is critical to the success of your paper, so don't skimp on your editing and polishing efforts.

Remember that a cardinal tenet in writing a research paper is to communicate your results to your reader. The next writing rule therefore stresses the importance of keeping your reader in mind as you write.

Writing Rule 7:
Be Reader Oriented

When writing and revising your paper, keep your reader in mind at all times. Make sure that your introduction explains clearly not only what your thesis and general results are but also why they are significant. Then make sure that your introduction serves its second—but equally important—function, which is to capture the reader's attention. The most important goal in all writing is to get, and hold, the reader's attention. Unless you engage the reader in your subject at the outset, no communication can take place. Therefore, make your introduction interesting in whatever way you can—with a provocative or controversial statement, a humorous insight, or a concept that tantalizes the reader to continue reading.

When you are satisfied that your opening section will get your reader's attention, then you need to concentrate on holding that attention. Topic sentences are a must in clarifying for your reader what you are discussing in each paragraph. Keep your reader in mind as you move from paragraph to paragraph—let him or her know where you've been and where you're going with effective transitions. Similarly, at the end of major sections of your paper, pause for a moment. Use a sentence or two to summarize what you have been discussing and what you will be looking at next. If your paper is lengthy (over twelve pages or so), consider using subheadings to cue the reader to the content of each subsection.

A good conclusion to your paper is nearly as important as a successful introduction. Once you have said all you have to say about your subject, end the discussion. Conclude your paper. Summarize briefly for the reader your major points, or draw together the separate strands of your argument into a conclusive statement about your subject. Keep your conclusion brief and succinct, and strive to phrase your conclusion in a striking, memorable way. Remember, the conclusion is the last thing your reader will read about your subject.

A clear introduction, topic sentences, effective transitions, and a conclusion that pulls the parts of your paper together—these are the basics of a successful research paper. Once these basics are present, then concentrate on furthering your communicative efforts by applying the remaining writing rules.

Writing Rule 8:
Use Your Own Words

Your writing will be more effective—and a much easier undertaking—if you express your ideas and conclusions in your own words, just as you would if you were telling someone about your project. After spending weeks in the library immersed in documents, data, and various scholarly works, it may be difficult to remember that it is you, and not Scholar A or Scholar B, who is writing the paper. Whenever you catch yourself imitating another's style or using words or phrases that you would not ordinarily use in conversation, ask yourself how you would explain whatever point you are trying to make to a friend. Explain it out loud, just as if your friend were there beside you. Then write down what you have said. In general, write as if you were speaking. Use the kind of words that you would use when talking to another. If you don't routinely use such terms as "moreover" or "indeed" or "however" in your conversations, don't use them very often when writing.

Similarly, avoid using technical, field-specific terminology. Nearly every area of study has its attendant jargon and often highly specialized vocabulary. If it is necessary to use such terms in your writing, make sure that you define them clearly for your reader and use them consistently. If possible, avoid them. Take particular pains to avoid the kind of language used in government documents and memoranda—which can rise to dizzying heights of noncommunication. This may require substantial translating ability on your part. Consider, for example, the following government directive, which was issued to government personnel in 1942 in the midst of World War II:

> Such preparations shall be made as will completely ob-
> scure all Federal buildings and non-Federal buildings
> occupied by the Federal government during an air raid for
> any period of time from visibility by reason of internal or
> external illumination.

When President Franklin Roosevelt was told that government employees could not decipher the meaning of the memo, he did his best to clarify the message: he informed his aide to "Tell them that in buildings where they have to keep the world going to put something across the windows." Although FDR's prose in this instance was not memorable, it did serve to communicate the message. The point is, communication comes first; and this can best be achieved by using your own words.

Also, avoid using too many quotations. If you can paraphrase in your own words the content of a quotation just as effectively, do so. Quotations interrupt the flow of your text. Furthermore, your reader is primarily interested not in what your sources know but in what you have learned from them and how they relate to your thesis. Of course, if a quotation is particularly apt or illuminating of the point you are making, use it. A particularly apt quotation in the context of this paragraph is the following, from Ralph Waldo Emerson: "I hate quotations. Tell me what you know." Remember to identify your sources to the reader. If you use a direct quotation from an author, be sure to give the appropriate citation in the style—footnote, endnote or in-text citation—preferred by your instructor. If you discuss a theory or the results produced by another scholar, provide a citation to that work. Not giving credit for ideas or words is academic dishonesty and, if extreme, is considered plagiarism.

Writing Rule 9: Be Direct and to the Point

When writing your paper, be direct and to the point. Let your reader know exactly what you think and why, and express your thoughts in clear, simple language. If a smaller word works as well as a longer term, use it. For example, avoid saying *utilize*—say *use* instead. Similarly, say *because* rather than *due to the fact that; now* rather than *at this point in time* or *at this juncture; help* or *ease* rather than *facilitate; first* rather than *initial; rest* rather than *remainder; about* rather than *approximately*; and so on. Avoid trendy terms (seminal, paradigm, parameter, actualize, propensity, prioritize, vortex, etc.); they tend to confuse rather than clarify. Use short sentences that are easy for your reader to follow. Use the active voice ("The vice president accompanied the president") rather than the passive ("The president was accompanied by the vice president"). The active voice is more direct, easier to understand, more forceful, and generally less wordy.

As you write and revise your paper, keep in mind the five Ws (who, what, when, where, and why) of journalists and news reporters. Keep reminding yourself that your primary task is to communicate to the reader only the essentials. Use only that information that is *relevant* to your thesis. Very likely, only half—or even less—of the copious amounts of information you have gathered will actually be useful in writing your research paper. No matter how fascinating or illuminating in itself a certain quotation or item of information may be, if it is irrelevant to your topic, don't use it.

Writing Rule 10: Avoid Clutter

This writing rule is the counterpart of Writing Rule 9. Weeding the "clutter" out of your paper is simply another way to achieve the goal of direct communication with your reader. In revising your paper, look for and delete the following types of clutter:

1. Modifiers that are not essential for accuracy or clarity. Too many adjectives and adverbs can hide the "working words" (nouns and verbs) of your sentences.
2. Repetitious sentences or sections. Don't bore your reader with overstatements.
3. Unnecessary tables or illustrations. If you have included tables or illustrations in your paper, consider whether they are really necessary. Could you summarize in words the same information just as well?
4. Long, complex sentences. Use two—or more— shorter sentences instead.
5. Extraneous phrases, such as "I might add that" or "it should be pointed out that" or "it is important to note that."
8. Any irrelevant statement or information.

Writing Rule 11: Be Convincing

Imagine for a moment that you are an attorney in a courtroom defending a client's innocence. Your primary goal is not simply to tell the jury that your client is innocent, but to *convince* the jury of this fact. Similarly, in a research paper it is not sufficient to merely describe your topic and your conclusions to your reader. You need to support your conclusions with convincing evidence. Share significant sources with your reader. Describe them. Explain how they shed light on your topic and how they relate to your conclusions. Let your sources convince your reader, just as they convinced you.

Also, avoid using too many qualifiers when you present your evidence. Qualifiers are words and phrases such as *it would appear that, it seems, apparently, possibly, somewhat, perhaps, it may be that, it is often the case that*, and the like. When you are uncertain about an item of information or event, a qualifier is necessary to avoid misleading the reader. Too many qualifiers, however, tend to lead the reader to suspect that you are reluctant to support your own argument. A good research paper is convincing, and, to convince your reader, a firm commitment on your part is necessary. Your choice of words needs to reveal this commitment.

Writing Rule 12:
Pay Attention to Grammar and Style

When you are revising your paper, take time to look for grammatical errors. Check for noun-verb agreement, consistency in your use of tense, and split infinitives. Make sure that it is clear what word a modifier is modifying. Above all, check for correct spelling. Spelling errors are difficult to forgive because they can be so easily prevented. Misspelled words indicate carelessness and inattentiveness to the language—take pains to avoid them.

Evaluate your paper for its tone, or "sound" quality. Read it aloud, and listen to the ring of your words and sentences. Too many short sentences in a row will make your text sound choppy. To avoid this, vary the length of your sentences until they flow smoothly. Also evaluate your word choice. Have you used the same word repeatedly when a substitute is available? Check your thesaurus for vivid, precise equivalents.

A final note. Thoughtful writers today use gender-inclusive language. A senator must heed the desires not of *his* constituents, but of *his* or *her* constituents. Admittedly, using gender-inclusive language sometimes can result in awkwardness. One of the simplest ways to circumvent the problem is to use the plural instead of the singular—"senators must heed the desires of *their* constituents." In general, be inventive; rephrase your sentences until they read as smoothly as possible given this particular constraint.

Summary of Rules on How to Write a Successful Research Paper

1. Plan ahead when selecting your topic.

2. Develop a research strategy.

3. Create an outline before you write.

4. Use a word processor, if possible.

5. Remember—a first draft is only a first draft.

6. Allow plenty of time for revising.

7. Be reader oriented.

8. Use your own words.

9. Be direct and to the point.

10. Avoid clutter.

11. Be convincing.

12. Pay attention to grammar and style.